Butterflies To Breakups

The life cycle of love

Esha Kak

Made with ❤ on the BookLeaf Publishing Platform
www.bookleafpub.in
www.bookleafpub.com

Dedication

For my mother, who thinks I'm the best poet in the world, my father, who always strives for the best version of himself, and my daughter, my lifeline.
And my best friend Aakash, who knows these poems better than anyone else.

Preface

'Butterflies to Breakup' is my first book.

A beautiful drop in the sea of poems I have been writing since 2021, but never dared to let the world read.

The crushed pieces of my heart dissolved in my tears make the ink on these pages, dried up by the cozy, warm rays of insane optimism.

It is for all those madly in love to know that things change. Love goes through its ups and downs and sometimes, hearts break.

It is for all broken hearts to know, there will be love again.

Acknowledgements

All the words in this book belong to my wounded, eternally hopeful heart. I am a poet because of them. With all my heart, thank you to the ones it didn't work out with, and the future love they prepared me for.

1. No Excesses In Love

They say
Over-loving can kill a relationship
I ask them
Do they even know
What love is

2. What I Really Wanna Do

I want to smother you
With my love
Suffocate you
With kisses
Overwhelm you
With attention
But I'd rather not

3. Manifesting

A scribbled-on page
Is better than a blank one
And so I write
A love poem for us
Wishing it into reality

4. Hoping

Everyday
I wake up
And pick up my phone
Staring hard
With half open eyes
Hoping there will be
A message from you
Telling me
You still miss me

The daily cycle of life
Birth of a tear
And death of hope

5. Beautiful Ruins

All women
Have that one man
Who ruined them
For any other

6. Internal Wars

It seemed like we were
Meant to be
Nothing could shake
The fortress of love
We had built
Little realising
The enemies inside us
Were enough
To break it down

7. Amnesia

I have tried to understand
What went wrong
On some days
A lot comes to mind
And on others
I struggle
To think of anything
Did we make a mistake?

8. Unforgettable?

I try to slap that vision
Out of my head
You smiling
Blushing

My forehead
Misses your kisses

9. All Cried Out

When the pain gets too much
I cry
Let the pain flow
Let the choked throat ease out
It does help
Till pain strangles me again

10. The Twister

I reach out
But there's no hand to hold
And the forever stabbed knife in my chest
Starts twisting again
Does it happen to you too?

11. No Tea, Please

I haven't made tea
Since 'we' stopped being
Just coffee for me
Thank you!

12. Love...Again

Falling in love again
Takes courage
Weaponising someone
And hoping they won't
Riddle you with bullets
The old bullet wounds
Haven't healed yet

But I did

13. Don't Call Me

There are different stages of grief
Denial is the first
I keep waiting
For my phone to ring

14. Expectations

She wanted to give him
All the pieces of her
But he wanted
To stay whole

15. Lost, But Not Found

I went to the market
Looking for perfume
That smells like you
I got the bottle
But where do I find you?

16. Shameless

They say I have no shame
Baring my soul
Just like that
For everyone to see
I don't need to tell them
I'm just hoping
You
Read these poems

17. What A Bitch

I knew I was falling hard
I was falling deep
In love that flares
With all its might
And goes away quietly
Leaving no trace
What if it never ends?
The optimistic me
Is an intolerable bitch

18. Unsaid

Often
It's just words
Keeping people apart
Ones that were said
Or ones that weren't

19. Breakup Therapy

There's no temptation
Greater
Than that of writing
At 2am
Knowing it's the only thing
Helping me
Go back to sleep
And calming the crippling sadness
Of knowing
That I will never see you again

20. The calm to my hurricane

In my world
Of tree-ripping
House-shattering
Car-spinning
Hurricanes
You are the time
That calms

21. All About You

I write
And write
And then
I write some more
A lot about you
And a little
About me too

22. Dead Or Alive?

Did you know
Missing someone
Can make you feel
Like you're being hit
By a train
Repeatedly
Every second of
Every
Damn
Day

23. Un-deleted memories

Looking at our pictures
I wonder
Where did we go wrong?
Did we go wrong?
Or we thought we did
And messed things up
Ourselves
I try pressing the delete button
But I lock the phone
Again
And close my eyes

24. Don't Call Him!

I stare at your number
Watching the digits
Do their mocking dance
My fingers
Circling them
What will I say
If you do pick up
And I keep my dumb phone down
Yet again